The Story of Mother Tree

Jane Scoggins Bauld

Illustrations by Cynthia G. Darr

Book Design by Jonathan Maedche

Spring

A Coldwater Press Book
© 1997 by Jane Scoggins Bauld.
All rights reserved. Published in the U.S.A. by
Coldwater Press, Dallas Texas.

Library of Congress Catalog Card Number: 97-68119

The Story of Mother Tree tells the true narrative of
Isamu Taniguchi's gift of a garden to the people of Austin, Texas,
and how Mother Tree helped him.
[1. School stories; 2. Horticulture; 3. Non-fiction.]

ISBN 1-880384-12-4.

Dedicated to my husband Nathan,
who is my confidant and encourager.

A Word from the Author

During Isamu Taniguchi's lifetime he was awarded the Medal of Peace by the Emperor of Japan. The garden described in this book tells how he came to build it and how it helps everyone who visits it.

Mr. Taniguchi is no longer with us, but as we pause in our busy world, we can feel his spirit in the garden.

It helps others get back "in touch with the earth," which was one of Isamu Taniguchi's goals in life.

This true story of Mother Tree was told to me by Isamu Taniguchi himself. In it he explains how Mother Tree helped him build the garden.

I was honored to read the story to Isamu Taniguchi at the Harvest Moon Festival in the Bamboo Tea House before his death, and again to the children of Austin at his Memorial Service in the garden.

Enjoyment

樹

Tree

The Story of Mother Tree

Mother Tree grew on the side of a hill just outside the city.
Around her grew ferns and grasses, wild plums and blue ligustrum.

For many years Mother Tree stood alone, the largest tree on the
hillside. But one spring day someone came to sit beneath her
branches. He leaned against her trunk.

Mother Tree liked his touch.

She listened to the man's words. "If I build a garden it will take lots
of work. But what a garden it could be!"

"I can make a place for children to play, and for grown-ups to rest.
I can make a place for everyone to feel good about being here, and
to feel nicer toward each other."

So the man set to work. Using a long stick he sketched out plans
for the garden in the dirt.

Beginning

"I'll make the place to rest here,

and the place to play there.

I'll build a pond here,

and a bamboo forest there."

Mother Tree listened curiously as, into the twilight hours, Isamu Taniguchi mulled over plans for the garden he would build.

Finally the day came to put his shovel into the soil. It was time to start work on the garden!

There were weeds to pull,

and scrubby trees to clear away.

There were ancient rocks to be pried loose

from their embedded place in the soil.

But first must come the bamboo forest! This thick forest would make the garden a private place. In the coming fall Isamu would harvest the bamboo canes and use them to build the Bamboo Tea House in the middle of the garden.

Cultivation

Then there were ponds to dig!

"Can I really do all this?" he asked himself.

"Yes, you can do it," Mother Tree answered. "Just keep working. You can do it."

Isamu was surprised at Mother Tree's interest when he heard her speak to him, but at her urging he resumed his work.

Once the weeds were pulled Isamu chopped the small cedar trees with his ax. He saved their trunks, bound them tightly together, and laid them aside for the arched bridge he would build over one of the ponds.

"These will be the 'Bridge-to-walk-over-the-moon,'" Isamu declared.

His master plan was to create ponds to spell

Bridge

The last pond would be a quiet island in the shape of a ship, with an anchor of steppingstones for children to step across to watch Japanese koi play hide-and-seek among the lotus plants.

Each day Isamu worked from daylight to dusk. At midday he sat under Mother Tree to eat his lunch. As he took out his basket of food, he talked with her about his work for the day, and of his plans for tomorrow.

He leaned against her sturdy trunk, closed his eyes, and dreamed of the finished garden.

Mother Tree was happy to have him lean against her. She gladly gave him her shade and she always talked to him! Each day her branches whispered,

    "Keep going. Don't stop.

      Keep going. Don't stop."

Rest

As she spoke to him her breezes cooled his tired body. Isamu soon grew to love his Mother Tree, and to depend on her for companionship and encouragement.

Day after day she told him to keep digging, especially on days when he was ready to give up! "It's too much work!" he complained.

"Don't stop. Keep going," she repeated.

So Isamu kept working.

Summer and winter he worked, for all of one year and half of another! Many days he spent kneeling on the ground, loosening soil for planting.

Early spring rains kissed the plants and they grew. Bees and butterflies came to see what was going on. Birds perched on Mother Tree's branches and sang songs for Isamu from sunup till sundown.

Mother Tree blessed Isamu.

And she would not let him quit!

At last the ponds were dug. They were ready to be filled with water.

Garden

With a touch of Isamu's hand, water came tumbling across ferns and moss-covered rocks, cascading down from unknown places into the ponds Isamu had dug.

The rushing water used all its energy in the falls. By the time it reached the ponds it was deep and still.

The gurgling sound of the falling water was healing.

The stillness of the ponds was calming.

Along the borders of the ponds Isamu planted cherry tree saplings sent to him from along the Potomac River in Washington D.C. Their pink blossoms would welcome springtime year after year.

Each detail Isamu attended to as he worked to finish the garden — stone upon stone, plant upon plant. And then one day when the garden was almost finished, Isamu sat under Mother Tree for the last time.

The ponds were filled with water.

The flowers were bursting with blooms.

The Bamboo Tea House was complete, and

"The-Bridge-to-walk-over-the-moon" was in place.

Sorrow

Isamu waited for Mother Tree's encouragement. But today Mother Tree did not speak to him. She would never speak to him again, for when the garden was finished Mother Tree died!

Her work was done. She had given Isamu shade.

She had given him cool breezes.

And she had refused to let him quit!

Now her work was over. Isamu wept for her. His tears sank down to her deepest roots, but she did not come back to life. His dear, dear Mother Tree was dead.

Isamu built a pagoda beside her to honor her. "I will love you forever, Mother Tree. Without your help I could never have done it!"

And now today as Isamu leans against his shovel and wipes his brow with a towel, he looks across the garden. He knows he has done what Mother Tree wanted — he has finished the garden!

"I wish you could see it, Mother Tree," he whispered.

Completion

Today visitors come to the garden to see the ponds, and the Bamboo Tea House, and the quiet island in the shape of a ship. Children play on the steppingstones, and walk across the arched bridge. Grownups stop to rest beside the waterfalls and feel a surge of peacefulness when they leave.

All who pass Mother Tree's gnarled trunk remember how she gave herself for the garden. They see the pagoda built to honor her, and they can honor her, too.

This garden is a gift from Isamu Taniguchi and his beloved Mother Tree. Thank you, Taniguchi-san. Thank you, Mother Tree-san.

> "It is my wish that you have pleasant communion
> with the spirit of the garden."

Isamu Taniguchi (December 1897 - February 1992)